WHAT'S INSIDE?
TANKS

Peter Mavrikis

PowerKiDS
press.

WHAT'S INSIDE?
TANKS

Peter Mavrikis

PowerKiDS press™

Published in 2016 by The Rosen Publishing Group, Inc.
29 East 21st Street, New York, NY 10010

Cataloging-in-Publication Data
Mavrikis, Peter.
Tanks / by Peter Mavrikis.
p. cm. — (What's inside?)
Includes index.
ISBN 978-1-5081-4619-3 (pbk.)
ISBN 978-1-5081-4620-9 (6-pack)
ISBN 978-1-5081-4621-6 (library binding)
1. Tanks (Military science) — Juvenile literature. I. Mavrikis, Peter. II. Title.
UG446.5 M39 2016
623.74'752—d23

Project Editor: Michael Spilling
Design: Brian Rust and Andrew Easton
Picture Research: Terry Forshaw

Photographs:
Art-Tech/Aerospace: 8, 11, 15, 19, 20, 24, 32, 35
Cody Images: 3, 7, 10, 12, 14, 18, 26, 27, 39, 40
Dreamstime: 6 (Oknebulog), 22 (Martin Spurny), 28 (Gator),
34 (Martin Spurny), 38 (Typhoonski)
Ukrainian State Archive: 23
U.S. Department of Defense: 16, 30, 31, 36, 42, 43, 44

Artworks:
All artworks are Art-Tech/Aerospace, except page 45 Amber Books Ltd.

Manufactured in the United States of America
CPSIA Compliance Information: Batch #BW16PK:
For Further Information contact Rosen Publishing, New York, New York at 1-800-237-9932

Contents

Mark V Male

The Mark V Male was developed by the British Army during World War I (1914–1918). It was an improved version of the earlier Mark models, which included the first tank ever built by the British, the Mark I.

The Mark V first entered combat during the final months of World War I. This latest addition to the war proved to be a powerful weapon against enemy defenses and machine gun positions.

Naval Guns

The Mark V tank was armed with two **modified** naval guns. The guns of the Mark V were located on the side of the combat vehicle. Each tank carried more than 200 **shells**. Later tanks had the gun barrel placed in a **turret** on top of the tank.

A key feature of a tank is its pair of continuous caterpillar tracks, which spread the vehicle's weight and help move it over rough and bumpy ground.

Armored Boxes

Tanks are protected with thick metal **armor**. The vehicle's armor helps **defend** the tank crew from enemy gunfire and **shrapnel**. The Mark V was covered in 16 mm (.62 inch) of armor in the front and 12 mm (.47 inch) on the sides. At the time,

tank armor was made of steel. While on the attack, **infantry** forces often used the tank for cover against the gunfire of the opposing army.

Tanks were originally called "landships" and were developed to end the stalemate caused by trench warfare.

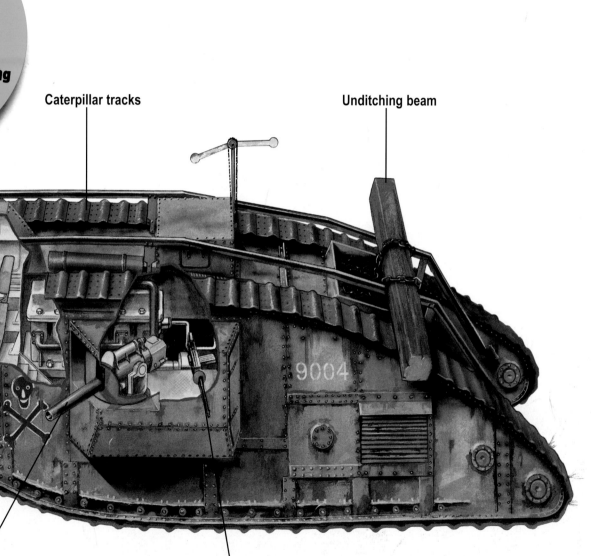

FACT

The Mark V had an eight-man crew including a commander, a driver, and six gunners.

Caterpillar tracks

Unditching beam

Driver

9004

Naval gun

Machine gun

Panzer VI Tiger

Referred to simply as the Tiger I, the Panzer VI was Germany's first heavy tank. It proved to be an effective opponent against the Soviet T-34 and U.S. M4 Sherman tanks. First developed in 1942, the Tiger played a major role in Germany's offensive strategies. It was considered the most powerful tank at the time.

Although the Tiger tank was impressive, building it was slow and costly. More than 1,300 Tiger tanks saw combat. Due to an unnecessary complicated design, production ended in the summer of 1944, almost a year before Germany surrendered.

Antiaircraft Gun

The tank's heavy offensive weaponry was an 88 mm (3.46-inch) converted antiaircraft gun. With its target sighting capabilities, the gun proved to be

Tiger tanks were first used against the Soviet army in the summer of 1942.

highly accurate when firing at enemy tanks. The gun could hit targets as far as 7,200 feet (2,010 m) away, allowing it to strike at the enemy while still beyond the range of their guns.

Combat King

The **hull** of the tank was protected by 100 mm (3.94-inch) metal armor. Still, few enemy weapons were able to **breach** the tank's defenses. Allied soldiers had to get close to the tank's side in

Deployed in units of around 50 tanks, Tigers were an impressive and deadly force.

order for antitank grenades to cause damage. The American-made Sherman tank needed to be within 330 feet (100 m) in order to penetrate the Tiger's armor, while the Tiger's antiaircraft gun was able to destroy enemy tanks as far away as 1,600 feet (500 m).

Did you know?

- **Tiger tanks were involved in combat across Europe and North Africa.**

- **During the Battle of Villers-Bocage, a single Tiger was able to destroy dozens of British Cromwell tanks whose own guns could not penetrate the Tiger's armor.**

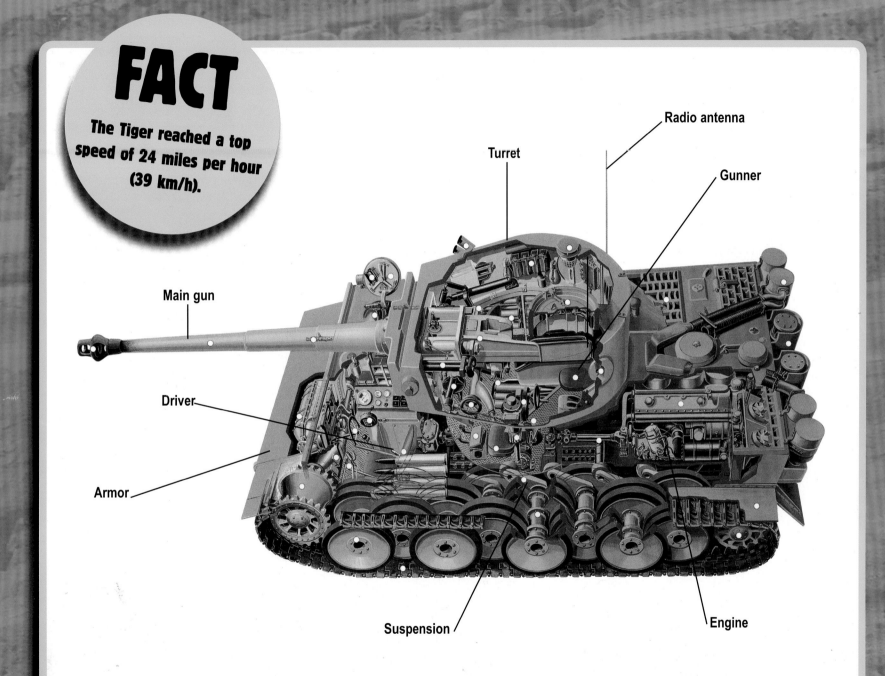

FACT

The Tiger reached a top speed of 24 miles per hour (39 km/h).

Radio antenna

Turret

Gunner

Main gun

Driver

Armor

Suspension

Engine

13

M4A4 Sherman

The Sherman tank was designed by the U.S. Army in response to Germany's effective armored units, which included both the Panther and Tiger tanks. Thousands of Sherman tanks were built during World War II and used by American, British, and Soviet forces across Europe and Africa.

Known as an effective main battle tank, Sherman tanks played a major part in the Allied invasion of mainland Europe, the Battle of the Bulge, and in the fall of Nazi Germany.

Battle Ready

The M4A4 tank's primary weapon was a 75 mm (2.95-inch) gun. Standard artillery rounds weighed

The M4A4 played a big role in the July 1943 Allied invasion of Sicily and in the invasion of Normandy in June 1944.

Great Expectations

The first Sherman tanks were sent to North Africa and fought in the Battle of El Alamein in October 1942. There they proved to be an effective **counter** to the German Panzer III. This early success, however, did not repeat a few years later when the Sherman faced off against heavier German tanks in Europe. The Tiger and later Panther models outmatched the Sherman, inflicting heavy losses.

Sherman tanks served many purposes. Some operated as enemy tank "killers," while others offered support to infantry, often providing cover against enemy fire.

14 pounds (6.32 kg). The M4A4 was mostly used in tank-to-tank combat. In addition to the main gun, Sherman tanks were also armed with two .30–caliber machine guns and one .50–caliber machine gun.

Did you know?

• A crew of five soldiers operated Sherman tanks.

• Unlike many of the earlier tank models, the M4A4 had **welded plate** or **cast armor** instead of bolted armor.

FACT

Sherman tanks could reach a maximum speed of 25 miles per hour (40 km/h).

.50-caliber machine gun

Main gun

Sloped armor

Gunner

Engine

Panzer V Panther

Germany's fifth panzer ("tank") in the series, the "Panther" played a key role during World War II (1939–1945). The Panther was used by Nazi Germany in battles across Europe and was favored for its mobility, armor defense, and firepower.

The Panther tank was created by the German Army to go up against the Soviet T-34 tank. Many of the battles involving the Panther took place along Europe's Eastern Front.

Rotating Turret

Unlike the earlier tanks of World War I, the tanks of World War II placed the cannon on top of the tank's main body—or hull—and in a rotating turret. The turret allowed the gunner to aim the tank's cannon in different directions without turning the entire tank. The main armament of the Panther tank was a 75 mm (2.95-inch) cannon.

The Panther played a key role in fighting against Soviet armor on the Eastern Front.

Sloped Armor

Few enemy weapons could pierce the Panther's thick front armor. Also, the hull design was slanted, which added to the tank's defenses by **deflecting** incoming fire. With a long barrel and powerful **ammunition**, the Panther was able to fire shells across great distances, often outperforming the field range of enemy tanks.

Panther tanks first entered combat in 1943 and fought against Soviet forces near the city of Kursk, in western Russia.

Did you know?

• Along with the Soviet T-34, many military historians consider the Panther as being one of the best tank designs of World War II.

• Almost 7,000 Panther tanks were built between 1943 and 1945.

FACT

In addition to its main gun, the Panther was also armed with two machine guns.

Turret

Engine

Main gun

Sloped armor

Suspension

T-34/85

Based on the smaller T-34/76, this Soviet-made tank was an improvement of the earlier version, armed with a more powerful main gun and stronger armor protection. Built in large numbers, these combat vehicles stopped Germany's advance into Russia and helped turn the tide of World War II along the Eastern Front.

A T-34/85 drives down a street somewhere in Germany, Spring 1945.

The T-34/85 first entered combat in late 1943. Throughout the war, the Soviet Union produced 40,000 models of this tank. Due to its successful design, the T-34/85 made up a large part of the Soviet armed forces during the early **Cold War**, which developed after the fall of Nazi Germany in 1945.

Did you know?

• **The T-34/85 was the chief tank in many Communist nations, and remains in service today in countries such as North Korea.**

• **Operation Citadel (July, 1943) was one of the biggest tank battles ever fought. An estimated 1,800 German tanks faced off against 3,600 Soviet tanks.**

Quantity versus Quality

The main weapon of the T-34/85 was its 85 mm (3.3-inch) gun that fired 19.8-pound (9 kg) rounds. Each tank carried up to 55 rounds of ammunition for the main gun. Although this tank did not match the firing range of the German-built Panthers and Tigers, the huge numbers of T-34/85 tanks produced provided a strong counter against the invading German forces.

In Combat

Built with added protection in mind, the armor of the hull was made of 90 mm (3.5 inches) of metal plating. However, this was still not enough to protect it from the deadly firepower of the German tanks. In head-to-head combat, a German Panther could destroy a T-34 before the Soviet tank had the chance to enter its own firing range.

A column of T-34/85 tanks park by the roadside during the winter of 1944–1945, during the final offensive against Nazi Germany.

FACT

By 1944, the Soviet Union had built more than 22,000 T-34/85 tanks.

Main gun

Commander's hatch

Engine

Driver

Suspension

Centurion A41

By the time the first Centurion A41 battle tanks came off the production line in January 1946, the war in Europe had come to an end. Nazi Germany was defeated the previous year. It did not take long, however, for the British-built Centurion to become a key weapon in the arsenals of many countries, including Canada, India, and Israel.

Weighing in at around 50 tons, the earlier models of the Centurion were criticized for being too slow and unable to travel long distances. The maximum range for these first models was 65 miles (104 km).

The Centurion tank has been used by the armies of many countries around the world, including Switzerland.

Firepower

Originally carrying a 85 mm (3.34-inch) main gun, later models included a 105 mm (4.13-inch) L7 gun with improved technologies that allowed for better targeting. The L7 gun alone weighed in at over 2,800 pounds (1,300 kg). Its main ammunition included armor-piercing shells designed to penetrate tank armor.

Did you know?

• The tank's engine is located behind a fireproof bulkhead made of welded steel.

• Centurion tanks served with Australian forces in the Vietnam War (1965–1973).

Worldwide Deployment

There have been over a dozen designs of the Centurion operated by different nations. Although it never entered combat in Europe, the Centurion saw action in the Korean War, the Vietnam War, and in battles fought by Israel during the Arab-Israeli wars.

This Centurion has a dozer blade fitted to the front, which allows it to knock down obstacles.

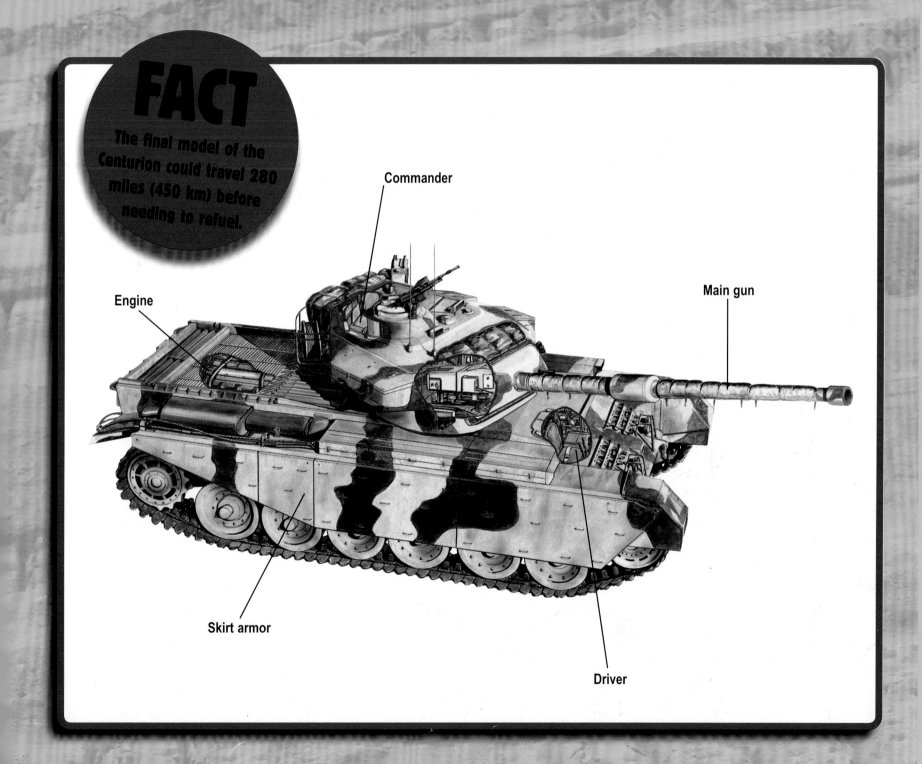

FACT

The final model of the Centurion could travel 280 miles (450 km) before needing to refuel.

Commander

Engine

Main gun

Skirt armor

Driver

T-72

This Soviet-era tank first entered production in the early 1970s. It is estimated that more than 30,000 T-72 tanks have been built. With the exception of the 9,000 tanks kept by the Russian Army, the rest were sold to other nations, including the Warsaw Pact countries of Poland, Hungary, and Romania.

● ● ● ● ● ● ● ● ● ●

The T-72 is considered a medium tank and is similar to the earlier T-64, which began service in the early 1960s.

Rate of Fire

The T-72 is armed with a 125 mm (4.92–inch) **smoothbore** gun. Fitted with an automatic loader, the gun is able to fire an average of eight rounds a minute. When manually loaded, the rate of fire

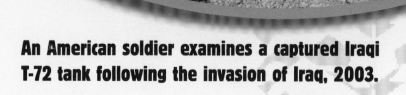

An American soldier examines a captured Iraqi T-72 tank following the invasion of Iraq, 2003.

31

is reduced to two rounds per minute. **Stabilizers** allow the gun to fire accurately at targets while the tank is in motion. Maximum shooting range is about 6,600 feet (2,000 m).

The T-72 was the main battle tank used by Iran during the Iran–Iraq War (1980–1988).

Did you know?

• As part of its defenses, the T-72 can release a smoke screen to either cover its retreat or confuse the enemy of its movements.

• The T-72 is operated by a three-person crew consisting of a commander, gunner, and driver.

Combat History

A number of countries in North Africa and the Middle East, including Syria, Iraq, and Libya, have the T-72. In the 1980s, the T-72 was used with deadly effect by Iraq against Iran's Chieftain tanks. In 1982, Syrian T-72 tanks faced off against Israeli defenses in Lebanon. In the First Gulf War (1990–1991), U.S. Abrams tanks proved better armed and armored than the T-72. More recently, T-72s have seen action in Chechnya (2009) and in Syria's civil war, which started in 2011.

FACT

The T-72 is currently in service in around 40 countries, including China, Venezuela, and Finland.

Machine gun

Gunner

Driver

Main gun

Sloping front armor

Leopard 2

A successor of the German-made Leopard 1, the Leopard 2 began its service in the West German army in 1979. An estimated 3,200 Leopard 2 tanks were built, with most sold to other NATO countries, including Canada, the Netherlands, Spain, and Turkey.

Developed in the middle of the Cold War, the Leopard 2 helped bolster NATO's defenses against the Warsaw Pact. At the time, the T-72 was the main battle tank used by the Communist nations of the Eastern Bloc.

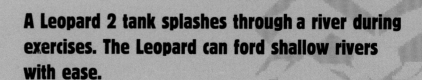

A Leopard 2 tank splashes through a river during exercises. The Leopard can ford shallow rivers with ease.

Mine Detectors

In addition to its many layers of armor, the latest Leopard 2 tanks were built with a mine-detection system. This allows the tank crew to avoid buried land mines. Leopard 2 tanks also have fire defenses and are capable of withstanding chemical, biological, and nuclear threats.

This Leopard tank is covered in camouflage made up of bits of tree. The camouflage helps the tank hide from enemies when in woods and forests.

On the Move

The tank's main armament is a 120 mm (4.72–inch) smoothbore gun. The Leopard 2 can fire accurately on enemy targets while traveling over rugged **terrain**. The tank's gun fires armor-piercing shells. Each tank can carry more than 40 rounds of main ammunition. A roof-mounted machine gun can engage enemy infantry as well as low-flying aircraft.

Did you know?

• The Leopard 2 was built with an escape hatch located in the floor of the tank.

• Leopard 2 tanks have a crew of four, including a commander, driver, loader, and gunner.

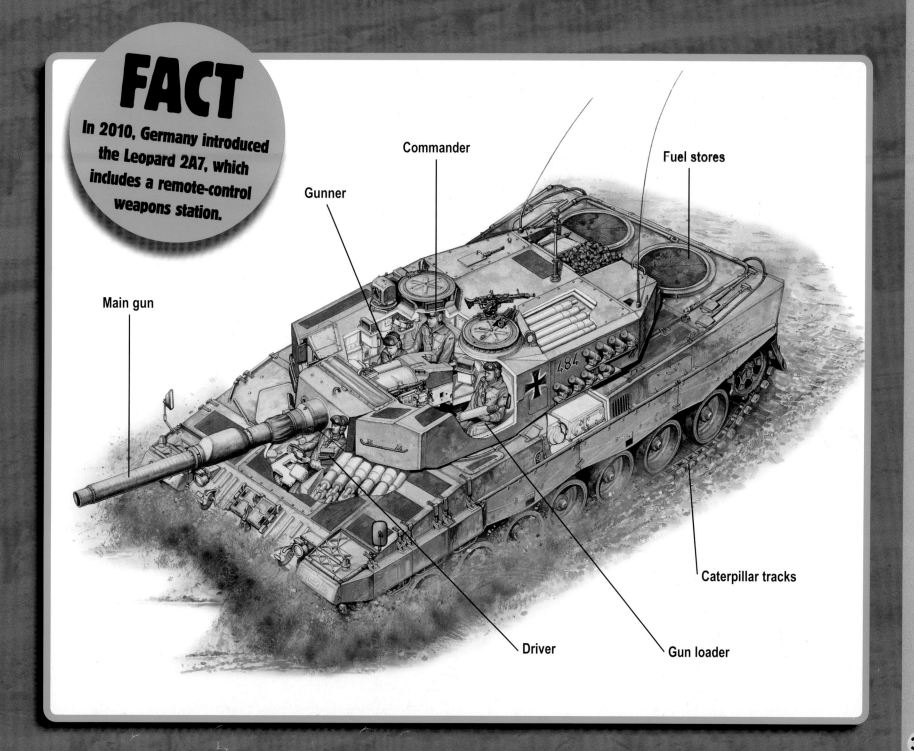

FACT

In 2010, Germany introduced the Leopard 2A7, which includes a remote-control weapons station.

Commander

Fuel stores

Gunner

Main gun

484

Caterpillar tracks

Driver

Gun loader

CHALLENGER 1
CLIMBING ON
THIS VEHICLE IS
STRICTLY FORBIDDEN

CHALL
CLIMB
THIS V
STRICTLY

Challenger 1

The Challenger 1 Is a British-built tank, which entered service in 1983. It has seen action in the Middle East during Operation Desert Storm, as well as in Bosnia and Herzegovina as part of a United Nations military force.

Originally modeled after the Chieftain tank, the Challenger has a number of upgrades, including a more powerful engine. It has advanced armor protection, providing it with a high level of defense against antiarmor artillery.

This British Challenger 1 tank was on patrol in the Balkans during peacekeeping operations in the 1990s.

Deadly Impact

The Challenger 1 was originally armed with a 120 mm (4.72-inch) L11A5 gun. This main gun was later replaced with the L30 gun, allowing it to fire armor-piercing rounds with depleted uranium warheads. These munitions are very effective and cause huge damage to their targets.

Weighing in at close to 70 tons, the Challenger is one of the heaviest tanks ever built.

Did you know?

• With the addition of a bulldozer plate, Challenger 1 tanks can also serve in mine-clearing operations.

• The exact makeup of Chobham armor is classified. The same type of armor is also used in the American M1A1 Abrams tank.

Superior Armor

Challenger tanks are equipped with **Chobham armor**, an extremely hard protective ceramic plating that can deflect explosive antitank rounds. The sloped design of the turret and front armor add to its **ballistic** defense. In addition to its superior armor, metal skirts on the sides add extra protection to the tracks and underside section.

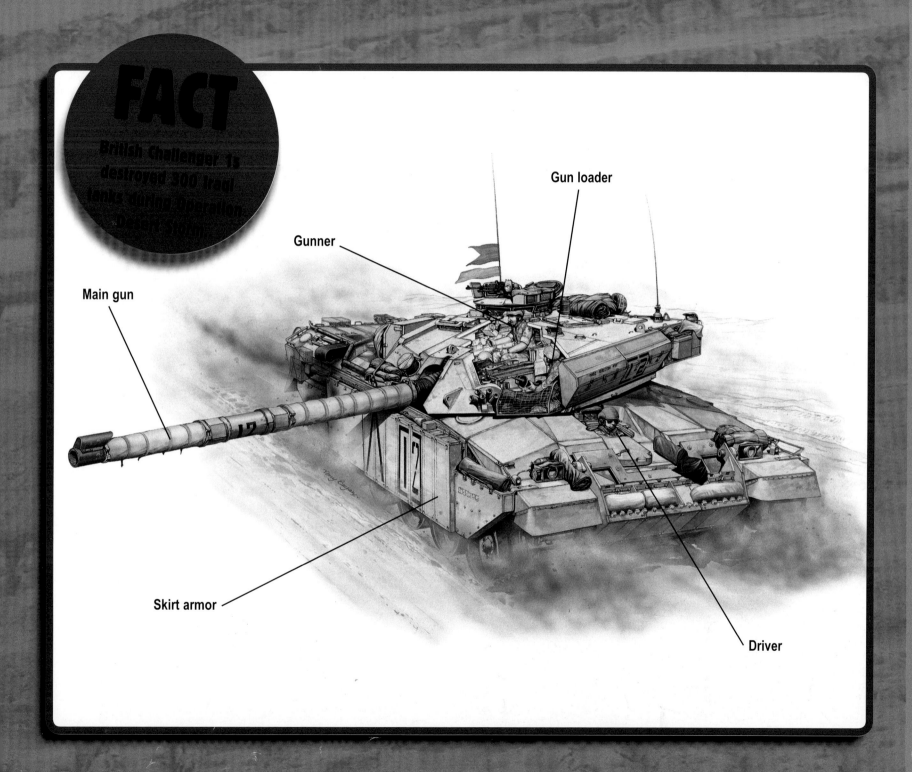

FACT

British Challenger 1s destroyed 300 Iraqi tanks during Operation Desert Storm.

Gun loader

Gunner

Main gun

Skirt armor

Driver

M1A2 Abrams

This American tank was named after U.S. Army general and chief of staff Creighton W. Abrams Jr. (1914–1974). The M1A2 Abrams is a well-armed, highly mobile, and heavily armored tank. First built in 1985, thousands of these tanks are in service around the world. The Abrams is currently used as the main battle tank by the U.S. Army.

Though first built in the 1980s, the Abrams tank did not see combat until Operation Desert Storm, which was launched against Iraq in 1991.

An M1A2 Abrams tank is unloaded from the back of a tank transporter.

Maximum Protection

Capable of destroying moving targets and enemy defenses, the M1A2 also provides its four-member crew with a high level of protection against hostile fire. Current models have more than 27 inches (686 mm) of hull armor. The tank is also protected against chemical, biological, and nuclear weapons. In the event of a successful direct strike or accident, the ammunition is safely stored in a "blowout" compartment.

This Abrams tank is camouflaged in a green and brown pattern.

Top Gun

The tank's main firepower comes from a 120 mm (4.72–inch) smoothbore gun that has the ability to fire on an enemy as far away as 13,000 feet (4,000 m). This gun can fire several different types of ammunition, but the main shell is the armor-piercing round. The Abrams also carries three machine guns.

Did you know?

• **Many NATO nations and other U.S. allies have Abrams tanks serving in their militaries.**

• **The main gun of the M1A2 can fire up to ten rounds a minute.**

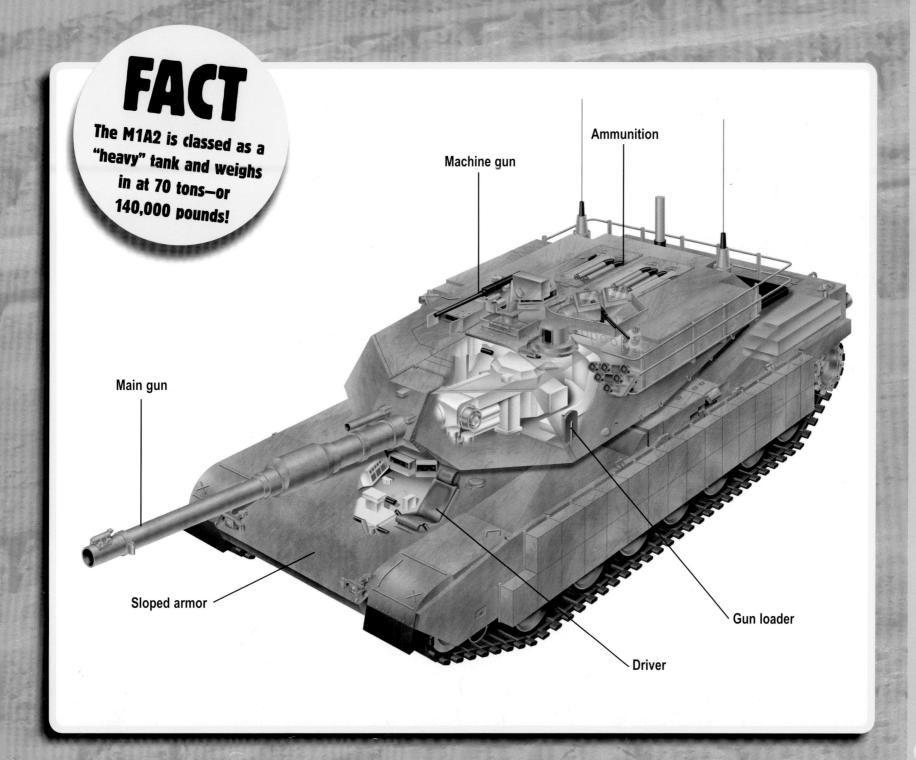

FACT

The M1A2 is classed as a "heavy" tank and weighs in at 70 tons—or 140,000 pounds!

Machine gun

Ammunition

Main gun

Sloped armor

Driver

Gun loader

Glossary

ammunition — material used to attack or defend against an enemy

armor — protective covering

arsenal — a collection of weapons

ballistic — dealing with missiles or projectiles

breach — to break through

bulkheads — walls that separate the different sections of a tank

Chobham armor — a very strong armor consisting of multiple layers of extremely hard ceramic tiles and metals

classified — kept secret

Cold War — the period after World War II known for tense relations between the United States and the Soviet Union

counter — to act against

defend — to protect

deflect — to bounce off

engineering — the building of useful machines

firepower — the strength of military weapons

hull — the outer body of a tank

infantry — soldiers that fight on foot

mobility — having the ability to move easily

models — types

modified — changed to serve a different purpose

NATO — a defense alliance between the United States, Canada, and many European countries

offensive — relating to an attack

retreat — to leave a battle

shell — a projectile for a cannon

shrapnel — pieces of an exploding mine or artillery shell

smoothbore — gun barrels that are "smooth" and do not have ridges and grooves of the kind found in "rifled" barrels

stabilizer — the device that keeps a tank's gun steady or stable when firing on targets

terrain — type of ground or land

trench warfare — fighting strategy of World War I where long dug-in positions were used for defense and as staging points for attacks

turret — the rotating structure on a tank that holds the main gun

Warsaw Pact — an alliance formed between the Soviet Union and the countries of Eastern Europe

welded — metal joined together through the process of heating

Index